NO PAIN, NO GAIN:
TAXES, PRODUCTIVITY, AND ECONOMIC GROWTH

A Twentieth Century Fund Paper

NO PAIN, NO GAIN

Taxes, Productivity, and Economic Growth

Louis A. Ferleger and
Jay R. Mandle

The Twentieth Century Fund Press/New York/1992

The Twentieth Century Fund is a research foundation undertaking timely analyses of economic, political, and social issues. Not-for-profit and nonpartisan, the Fund was founded in 1919 and endowed by Edward A. Filene.

Library of Congress Cataloging-in-Publication Data

Ferleger, Lou.
    No pain, no gain : taxes, productivity, and economic growth / by Louis A. Ferleger and Jay R. Mandle.
        p.   cm.
    "A Twentieth Century Fund paper."
    Includes index.
    ISBN 0-87078-346-7 : $9.95
    1. Taxation--United States. 2. Government spending policy--United States. 3. Public investments--United States. 4. Industrial productivity--United States.   I. Mandle, Jay R.   II. Title.
    HJ2381.F45   1992   92-42839
    336.2'00973--dc20   CIP

Cover Design: Claude Goodwin
Manufactured in the United States of America.

FOREWORD

D uring the decade of the 1980s, the glamour and scope of financial markets and financial "deals" masked the fact that they seldom addressed the issues of real economic growth. In fact, since 1973, productivity growth in the United States has been relatively sluggish. In the past dozen years, four-fifths of American workers suffered declines in real wages; more single-earner families became impoverished; and income distribution became more unequal. Our children perform poorly on tests of science and math; our products face increasing international competition; and our savings rate is near the bottom among industrialized countries. Our infrastructure is deteriorating faster than it is being maintained or replaced. The long-term solutions to all these problems, of course, are rooted in training, innovation, and investment. But there remains considerable uncertainty about what mix of public policies affecting taxes, incomes, and spending will contribute the most to ensuring the success of any solution.

This uncertainty about how to deal with the economic problems facing us is the subject of widespread public debate that seems to be taking place on two levels. At one extreme, as manifested in the recent presidential election, the public was willing to take seriously someone who claimed that the mere application of common sense could clear up the problem in a week or two. In addition to this kind of political "doctoring," we are routinely offered surefire solutions by ideologues of the free market and the "public" class of academics. The other side of the coin is a continuing, thoughtful, although unresolved dialogue on the subject by serious and objective scholars. Their work is providing keys to understanding the difficult issues involved and may hint at possible policy responses.

The discourse of the scholarly community differs from that of the first group by its restraint: few claim that a ready prescription is waiting for us at a nearby Washington drugstore. The participants in these ongoing discussions admit that their uncertainty is great, and they work hard to remain open to new findings. Both the public and the academic conversations are very important. Breakthroughs will come, as they always do, from the occasional merging of the two streams—a flash of insight translated into the rough approximation of the idea in the form of public policy. Such a moment cannot come too soon.

The circumstances, causes, and remedies of our disappointing economic performance have been the subject of a number of Twentieth Century Fund projects. We have sponsored, and are continuing to sponsor, books, papers, and task forces looking at various aspects of this broad problem. Herbert Stein looked at the way America spends (*Governing the $5 Trillion Economy*) and B. Douglas Bernheim looked at the way Americans save (*The Vanishing Nest Egg*); Murray Weidenbaum explored defense spending (*Small Wars, Big Defense: Paying for the Military After the Cold War*) and Jacques S. Gansler is embarking on an examination of defense conversion; James L. Pierce looked at America's banking policy (*The Future of Banking*) and Otis L. Graham, Jr., looked at America's industrial policy (*Losing Time: The Industrial Policy Debate*); we set up task forces to look at trade policy (*The Free Trade Debate*), economic policy (*Partners in Prosperity*), and market speculation and corporate governance. Moving ahead, we are looking at privatization, capitalism, and management leveraged buyouts.

Our goal is to help broaden the understanding of the issues, the only road to wise decisionmaking in the public policy arena. In the paper that follows, several of the key policy questions central to the ongoing economic debate are analyzed. Louis Ferleger and Jay Mandle examine the implications of current trends in thinking about overall tax burdens and tax progressivity for savings, investment, and productivity. Their analysis should help revive the debate about the effects of these public sector policies on long-term economic growth. On behalf of the Trustees, I thank them for their efforts.

Richard C. Leone, *President*
The Twentieth Century Fund
November 1992

CONTENTS

ACKNOWLEDGMENTS

Many people have helped, provided sources, and reviewed earlier drafts of this paper. We would like to thank James Cronin, Stanley Engerman, Thomas Ferguson, Elizabeth Fox-Genovese, Eugene D. Genovese, Carol Ivan, William Lazonick, Joan D. Mandle, Jon Mandle, Isadore Reivich, Jim Shoch, Robert Solow, Richard Sylla, and Robert Turner for their advice and comments. We also are very grateful for the suggestions of Richard Leone, John Samples, Bernard Wasow, and Matthew Leish.

Research assistance was provided by Paul Shik Lee, Jr., Wayne Hatmaker, and Daniel Lipstein.

THE ARGUMENT

Americans are tax averse. Much of the political dynamic in our country in recent years has been driven by that hostility to taxes. But although our tax burden is low when compared to that of the citizens of other advanced nations, this seemingly enviable position is accompanied by a failing economy and low productivity growth. The reasons for our tax aversion seem to lie in a resentment of the way taxes are collected and the uses to which tax money is put. The time, however, may be ripe for a change, especially given the tenor of the 1992 presidential campaign. This paper will explore the reasons behind, the problems caused by, and the possible solutions to American attitudes toward taxation.

Our productivity growth currently lags behind that of Japan and the most advanced members of the Organization for Economic Cooperation and Development (OECD). This gap is caused, in part, by the United States undertaxing itself and therefore insufficiently engaging in public investment. When the ratio in the United States of taxes collected to gross domestic product (GDP) is compared to the ratio found in other countries, and when the public sector investment rate (capital outlays by government at all levels) is taken as a percentage of total output, it is evident that both the tax burden and the rate of public-sector investment in the United States are lower than in the comparison countries.

The implication of this low ranking is magnified by the consideration that there has been a strong and statistically significant relationship in recent years between the growth in tax burdens and productivity growth. The country in which productivity growth was greatest, Japan, was also the country in which the increase in tax burden was the highest. Conversely, in the United States, where the growth in tax burden was least, productivity growth was the lowest. These data suggest that the actual relationship between productivity growth and changes in a country's tax burden may be the direct opposite of conventional wisdom. Rather than taxation and public spending being harmful to productivity growth, the evidence suggests that, on the contrary, it is helpful.

Evidence of a positive relationship between increases in tax revenues and productivity growth does not indicate the direction of causality. Though this paper argues that more rapid increases in tax ratios and resulting public investment were responsible for higher productivity growth in countries other than the United States, the reverse causal flow is also possible. In fact, both probably occurred. However, because the contribution the public sector can make to increase the productivity of an economy has received very little attention in this country, this paper emphasizes its causal role.

To investigate the reasons that the United States undertaxes itself compared to its competitors, it is necessary to consider the kind of taxes that are usually implemented, the degree of progressivity of each country's income tax, and the pattern of public-sector expenditures undertaken. In general, the situation in the United States differs considerably from that in Japan and the OECD countries, and these differences may hold the clue to why we tax ourselves relatively little. With regard to revenue, the United States resorts to property taxes more than the other countries, and our income tax is substantially less progressive. The first is universally an unpopular tax, and the degree to which the second is acceptable seems to be related to its progressivity. Thus the United States taxes precisely in a way that triggers the greatest hostility. In addition, our pattern of public expenditures may be a source of our reluctance to tax ourselves. The very heavy level of U.S. defense expenditures and the low levels of outlays on health, education, and infrastructure may signal trouble in terms of popular support; the benefits that are derived from such spending are not wide enough or apparent enough to mobilize a supporting constituency. If true, these hypotheses suggest that the low levels of taxation and public spending in the United States may not be the product of an ubiquitous antistate animus. Rather, it may be a reflection of the citizenry's disapproval of the way in which taxes are collected and of the uses to which their tax money is put.

The mismatch between government resource capabilities and capital spending patterns within the various tiers of the U.S. federal system may be another reason for inadequate educational and infrastructural expenditures. Public-sector investment is five times higher at the state and local level than at the federal level. The problem is that state and local governments are much less able to secure additional resources than the government in Washington. In recent years this has been made dramatically clear by the federal government's heavy reliance on borrowing, an option not open to most states and cities. At the same time, localities have been subject to political pressures much like those experienced at the national level to keep taxes low. Hence, at the level of government where most investment occurs, resources are rising very slowly.

The evidence uncovered in this paper suggests that, were we able to increase taxation, productivity would best be enhanced by improving the quality of education and augmenting the stock of public capital. Reversing the decline in capital outlays toward public education is necessary to overcome the failure of our educational system to keep pace with the requirements of modern technology. Similarly, spending on infrastructure must be matched to the requirements of modern technology in order effectively to advance productivity. It seems clear that such spending will have to be concentrated on the communications infrastructure necessary to support information-intensive industries.

The estimate given here is that to reverse the decline of the recent past and bring public-sector investment up to a reasonable level, such investment will have to increase by about 1.17 percent of the gross domestic product, representing approximately $60 billion. This money will have to be raised through taxation; therefore it is necessary to consider how such a tax package could be structured to secure the support of the people of this country. The principles that underlie such a tax proposal are that the United States make the tax structure more progressive, avoid raising the property tax, and minimize the use of the income tax, substituting a value-added tax (VAT) on consumption for any lost revenue. On the expenditure side, any additional revenues raised should be dedicated to education and public sector investment so that the taxpayers can observe the benefits of additional taxation.

The VAT's regressivity complicates matters. Therefore the introduction of a VAT must be counterbalanced by a dramatic increase in the progressivity of the federal income tax. This will be accomplished by exempting from income tax liability all taxpayers earning less than $25,000, reducing the tax liability of those earning between $25,000 and $50,000 by 25 percent, and increasing the income tax on those earning over $200,000 by 10 percent. These changes to the income tax in all would cost about $64 billion. This shortfall, in conjunction with the need to increase public investment by about $60 billion, will mean that close to $125 billion will have to be raised through the new VAT, requiring a VAT tax rate of about 7 percent.

There is reason for optimism that the kind of program suggested here will reduce the level of tax aversion present in the country. If the resulting growth in tax revenues is dedicated to education and infrastructure investment with the promise of a productivity payoff, the long-standing and debilitating hostility to taxation and to the public sector may be overcome. Public-sector investment will be seen for what it is—a contribution to increasing the economic well-being of the American people.

THE ANALYSIS

THE KEY TO COMPETITIVENESS: TOTAL FACTOR PRODUCTIVITY

In recent years, the productivity performance of the United States has been inferior to that of other developed countries. Figure 1 provides information on the annual increase in total factor productivity for the United States, Japan, and twelve other developed countries in the Organization for Economic Cooperation and Development (OECD). The data is structured in this way in order to make a dual comparison: the economic performance of the United States measured against one country (Japan) whose growth record universally is acknowledged to be excellent, and also compared to members of the OECD whose level of development is most similar to that of our own country.[1] Total factor productivity is an important indicator because it considers output to be a function of the principal inputs of production—capital and land as well as labor. It is the broadest and most reliable index of the extent to which an economy is increasing its efficiency in its use of productive resources. The rate of increase of total factor productivity is therefore the most important determinant of changes in a country's standard of living. The same measure also can be used as a yardstick of a nation's global competitiveness. Trends in factor productivity in one country over time and comparisons with other countries both provide important insight into a nation's economic well-being.

Looked at from either perspective, the experience of the United States in recent years has been unsatisfactory. Although its annual growth in total factor productivity between 1960 and 1973 averaged 1.6 percent, in the years since then its productivity performance has plummeted. Between 1973 and 1979 total factor productivity actually declined, while between 1979 and 1990 its growth was negligible at 0.3 percent annually. In each of the three time periods specified above, the United States lagged behind Japan

7

Figure 1
Average Annual Percentage Growth in Total Factor Productivity
United States, Japan, and OECD,*
1960-73, 1973-79, 1979-90

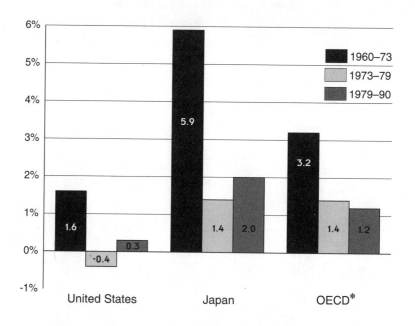

*Population-weighted mean for twelve OECD countries: Australia, Canada, Italy, United Kingdom, Germany, Austria, France, Belgium, Netherlands, Denmark, Sweden. Total factor productivity data for Norway are unavailable.

Source: Computed from Organization for Economic Cooperation and Development, OECD Outlook, no.50, Paris, December 1991, Table 48, p. 136; United Nations, Demographic Yearbook for the years 1966, 1981, and 1990 (New York: United Nations, 1967, 1983, 1992).

and the OECD countries. The gap with respect to the European countries has been consistently about 1.5 percent per year. Japan's superior performance has been even more evident. Recovering rapidly from destruction in World War II, that country's growth in total factor productivity sprinted in the 1960–73 period. But even in the 1973–79 and 1979-90 periods, when the Japanese rate had declined to more normal levels, that country's advantage in productivity gains was substantial.

CONSENSUS AND ALTERNATIVE EXPLANATIONS FOR SLOW U.S. PRODUCTIVITY GROWTH

These results, though dramatic, are not surprising. Most students of the U.S. economy agree that the pace of its productivity growth has been inadequate. What is surprising is that the reasons for this slow rate have not been fully identified. Writing in 1979, Edward Denison declared that "what happened [to cause the decline in productivity growth] is, to be blunt, a mystery."[2] More recently, John H. Bishop expressed a similar sentiment: "The absence of a rebound in multifactor productivity growth during the 1980s is particularly difficult to explain."[3]

Despite the agnosticism expressed by these scholars, a consensus has formed that identifies the nation's inadequate rate of saving and private investment as the principal source of the decline in productivity growth. The fact that the saving rate is lower in the United States than in comparable developed countries is indisputable; this is thought to be responsible for a lackluster level of private investment. Insufficient growth in the private capital stock is in turn believed to be responsible for a slowing in the rate at which new technology is introduced into production. One exponent of this generally accepted point of view is Charles Schultze, who has argued that the national savings rate should be 8 percent per year in order to permit living standards in the United States to grow by 1 percent per year. Such a target implies a substantial increase from the actual 2.5 percent rate of savings recorded between 1982 and 1990.[4]

This consensus view, however, does not stand up under close scrutiny. Were it valid, the decline in the rate of productivity growth should be associated with a similar fall in the share of the national resources devoted to private investment. Figure 2, however, which provides information on both the gross and net private investment rates grouped by years of economic expansion and contraction for the United States, suggests that such an association was present only for net investment and not for gross investment. Indeed, the table makes clear that since 1976 there has been an upward movement in the gross private investment rate. What accounts for this puzzling divergence in the trend of gross and net private investment rates? Which of the two is the appropriate measure to consider in determining the relationship between private investment and productivity growth?

The decline in net private investment in recent years can be explained by looking at the composition of investment in the 1970s. During these years private investment in buildings and structures declined relative to investment in equipment.[5] Such a shift typically produces a downward effect on the net investment rate because equipment is calculated to depreciate more rapidly than buildings. Between the time periods 1961–68 and 1983–88 gross private investment in equipment as a share of national income increased by almost 34 percent. During these same years, however, gross private investment in structures fell by 18 percent. These trends in themselves completely account for the discrepency between the net and the gross private investment rate. It is thus impossible to sustain the case that there has been a reduction in the allocation of resources devoted to private investment. The nature, not the level, of investment has changed.

Finding an explanation for the difference between the gross and net private investment rate does not by itself determine which one is the appropriate measure of the sources of productivity growth. Two considerations, however, point to the gross investment measure. The first concerns statistical accuracy. There are few economists who would argue that the depreciation schedules used to compute the net investment rate accurately correspond to the physical deterioration of plant and equipment. Rather, the schedules are devised and carried out for tax purposes. Thus it is very likely that the net investment statistic suggests a spurious precision in the computation of the wear and tear of plant and equipment. The resulting error is completely avoided in statistics that omit such deductions from their computation, like the gross investment statistic.

Perhaps even more important to consider is that investment in equipment seems to contribute more to productivity growth than does investment in structures. A recent study by J. Bradford DeLong and Lawrence H. Summers confirms that "equipment investment has far more explanatory power for national rates of productivity growth than other components of investment. . . ."[6] This suggests that the use of the net investment rate to measure investment's contribution to productivity growth is perverse. For according to this measure,

Figure 2
U.S. Gross and Net Fixed Nonresidential
Private Investment for all Industries
as a Percentage of National Income

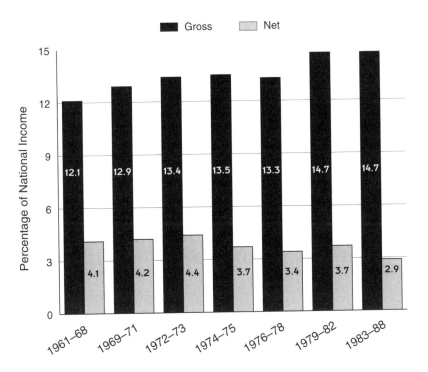

Source: Louis A. Ferleger and Jay R. Mandle, "Reverse the Drain on Productivity with Mass Education and Retraining," *Challenge* 33, no. 4 (July-August 1990), Table 2, p. 19.

a shift in the composition of investment toward productivity-raising equipment purchases causes a decline in investment, and a shift toward buildings and structures does the opposite.

Because of both its greater statistical accuracy and reliability in predicting productivity trends, therefore, the gross private investment rate is superior to the net private investment rate as an indicator of investment's contribution to productivity growth. And unequivocally, according to that better measure of investment, the decline in the productivity growth rate has not been associated with a fall in investment. Thus the central question remains: If a decline in private investment does not account for the fall in productivity growth, what does?

In recent years, David Alan Aschauer has taken up the hypothesis that a falloff in public-sector investment may make a major contribution in limiting the progress of productivity.[7] In a series of articles he has argued that if the rate of public investment in infrastructure had not declined the rate of productivity growth in the United States would have been much higher than it was. Aschauer's thesis has been the source of much controversy. In particular his estimates of the magnitude of the effect of declining investment in infrastructure on productivity have been widely questioned. Nonetheless, even a severe critic of the Aschauer thesis, Henry J. Aaron, has conceded that Aschauer "has called attention to the rather extraordinary disregard by economists and others of the possible role of public investment in explaining the slowdown."[8]

TAXATION AND PRODUCTIVITY GROWTH

One unexamined aspect of the issues raised by Aschauer is whether the productivity problem in this country is related to our tax structure. Specifically, there is a need to examine whether the volume and composition of taxation in this country has militated against high rates of productivity growth. Tables 1 and 2 present data on tax revenues as a percentage of the gross domestic product for the United States, Japan, and the twelve OECD countries considered in Figure 1. Expressing tax revenues as a percentage of the size of the economy is a way to consider the relative burden of taxation in each country or group of countries.

Table 1 indicates that over the period 1970 to 1989 the tax burden increased in each case. Japan's increase, however, was the most dramatic. Whereas the tax burden in 1970 in Japan was only 67.5 percent of that of the United States and 59.5 percent of that of the OECD grouping, by the

Table 1
Tax Revenues as a Percentage of
Gross Domestic Product, Selected Years,
1970–1989

	1970	1975	1980	1985	1989
United States	29.2	29.0	29.5	29.2	30.1
Japan	19.7	20.9	25.4	27.6	30.6
OECD[1]	33.1	34.6	37.0	39.0	39.5

[1] Population-weighted mean of Australia, Canada, Italy, United Kingdom, Germany, Austria, France, Belgium, Netherlands, Norway, Denmark, and Sweden.

Source: Computed from Organization for Economic Cooperation and Development, Revenue Statistics of OECD Member Countries, 1965-1990 (Paris: OECD, 1991), Table 3, p. 73.

Table 2
Tax Revenues, Excluding Social Security, as a
Percentage of Gross Domestic Product,
Selected Years, 1970–89

	1970	1975	1980	1985	1989
United States	23.6	21.9	21.8	20.6	21.3
Japan	15.3	14.9	18.0	19.3	22.1
OECD[1]	24.6	24.4	26.0	27.2	27.7

[1] Population-weighted mean of Australia, Canada, Italy, United Kingdom, Germany, Austria, France, Belgium, Netherlands, Norway, Denmark, and Sweden.

Source: Computed from Organization for Economic Cooperation and Development, Revenue Statistics of OECD Member Countries, 1965-1990 (Paris: OECD, 1991), Table 4, p. 74.

end of the period the share of GDP paid as taxes in Japan was marginally higher than in the United States and was up to 77.5 percent of that of the OECD nations. Over these years, in short, the Japanese tax burden grew the most while the United States tax burden grew the least. Indeed, between 1970 and 1985 the tax burden in the United States did not grow at all. During these same years the tax burden in Japan grew by 7.9 percentage points of GDP, or 40.1 percent, while in the OECD grouping the increase was 5.9 percentage points of GDP, or 17.8 percent.

In Table 2, where Social Security taxes are excluded, the pattern is even more clear. Over the entire period 1970 to 1989, the U.S. non-Social Security tax burden declined by 2.3 percentage points of GDP. In contrast, the OECD tax/GDP ratio increased from 24.6 to 27.7. The growth in this measure was even more dramatic in Japan, climbing from 15.3 to 22.1. Because of this trend, by the end of the period the United States had moved from a position in which its tax burden approximated that of the OECD and was substantially greater than that of Japan to one in which its tax burden was substantially less than in the OECD and slightly lower than in Japan.

Upon initial examination, there does not seem to be a clear relationship between the level of the tax burden and the growth in productivity. Through nearly all these years, Japan's tax burden was the lightest while its productivity growth rate was higher than the others'. Simultaneously, however, the OECD tax burden was higher than that in the United States; so too was its productivity growth.

There does appear to be a clear relationship, though, between the growth in the tax burden and advances in productivity growth (see Tables 3 and 4).[9] The country in which productivity growth was greatest, Japan, was also the country where the increase in the tax burden was the highest. The nation that saw its tax burden grow the least, the United States, also saw zero gain in productivity over the decade and a half. These data suggest, contrary to commonly held expectations, that productivity growth may be positively, not negatively, correlated with increasing tax burdens.

Confidence in the pattern that seems to emerge from the United States/Japan/OECD comparison is reinforced when the relationship between changes in the tax burden and the rate of productivity growth among the OECD countries themselves is examined. Tables 3 and 4 report on this relationship: the former includes social security taxes and the latter excludes them. When social security taxes are included there is a strong relationship among twelve of the countries (Sweden is the outlier). When social security taxes are excluded, a

Table 3
Average Annual Increase in
Total Factor Productivity, 1973-90, and
Increase in Tax Revenues as Percentage of
Gross Domestic Product, 1975-89

	Productivity Growth	Tax Revenue Increase
United States	0.0	1.1
Canada	0.5	2.9
Australia	0.7	2.5
Austria	1.0	2.4
United Kingdom	1.1	1.0
Netherlands	1.2	2.3
Germany	1.3	2.4
Denmark	1.3	8.5
Belgium	1.5	2.5
France	1.7	6.9
Japan	1.7	9.7
Italy	1.8	11.6
Sweden	0.6	12.5

Source: OECD Outlook, no. 50, Paris, December 1991, Table 48, p.136, and
Organization for Economic Cooperation and Development, Revenue Statistics of
OECD Member Countries, 1965-1990 (Paris: OECD, 1991), Table 3, p.73.

With Sweden omitted, r = 0.6763, statistically significant at the 0.05 confidence level.
r^2 = 0.4574

Table 4
Average Annual Increase in Total Factor Productivity, 1973–90, and Increase in Tax Revenues Excluding Social Security as Percentage of Gross Domestic Product, 1975–89

	Productivity Growth	Tax Revenue Increase
United States	0.0	-0.6
Canada	0.5	1.6
Australia	0.7	2.5
United Kingdom	1.1	0.7
Netherlands	1.2	0.3
Germany	1.3	0.5
Denmark	1.3	7.9
Belgium	1.5	0.6
France	1.7	2.7
Japan	1.7	7.2
Italy	1.8	11.1
Sweden	0.6	6.3
Austria	1.0	-0.7

Source: OECD Outlook, no. 50, Paris, December 1991, Table 48, p.136, and Organization for Economic Cooperation and Development, Revenue Statistics of OECD Member Countries, 1965-1990 (Paris: OECD, 1991), Table 4, p.74.

With Sweden and Austria omitted, r = 0.5659, statistically significant at the 0.05 confidence level. r^2 = 0.3202 statistically significant relationship exists when two outliers are removed (Sweden and Austria). Thus, the countries in which tax revenues as a share of GDP increased the most tended to experience higher rates of growth in total factor productivity than those in which the growth in tax revenues was relatively small.

Evidence of a positive relationship between increases in tax revenues and productivity growth does not, however, indicate the direction of causality. In principle, a rising tax/GDP ratio could either be the cause or the consequence of a relatively rapid increase in productivity growth. Indeed, one suspects that most economists would more likely assume that causality runs from productivity growth to the tax ratio rather than the other way around. Their argument would be that Japan and the OECD countries were able to increase taxes more than the United States was because their productivity performance was better and therefore their wealth grew faster. Not only is this argument plausible, but in all likelihood it contains a substantial degree of validity as well. All can agree that taxes are raised more easily when an economy is buoyant and growing rapidly than when it is in the doldrums. To advance this proposition, however, does not rule out the possibility that causality might flow in the reverse direction as well. While tax revenues may increase because of productivity growth, a larger public sector might contribute to that productivity growth in turn.

Raising taxes might stimulate productivity growth by permitting more public-sector capital formation.[10] If output is viewed as a positive function of both private and public investment, and each facilitates efficiency, then an increase in public capital would raise productivity to a level higher than it would be without such investment. It follows that a test of the hypothesis would be to see whether the countries where tax revenues as a percentage of gross domestic product grew the most were also the ones in which public-sector investment increased most rapidly. If so, then evidence would be at hand to suggest that causality ran from tax revenues to productivity as well as vice versa. The implicit argument is that when the government boosts its resources, productivity-raising public investment is facilitated.

Figure 3 displays data for the period between 1979 and 1989 for Japan, the United States, and the OECD countries.[11] The rate of public-sector investment is adjusted to hold constant the relative size of the public sector and thereby avoid exaggerating the investment performance of countries whose government is relatively large. These data tend to support the view that tax revenues facilitated productivity growth by encouraging public-sector capital accumulation. Japan increased tax revenues most dramatically

Figure 3

Increases in Tax Revenues as a Percentage of Gross Domestic Product, 1980–89

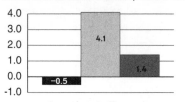

Increase in Taxes as
Percentage of GDP

Mean Gross Public Capital Formation as a Percentage of Gross Domestic Product, 1979–88

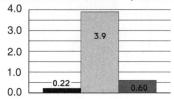

Gross Public
Investment Rate [1]

Mean Gross Private Capital Formation as a Percentage of Gross Domestic Product, 1979–88

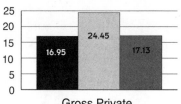

Gross Private
Investment Rate

[1] Adjusted public-sector capital formation rate calculated by multiplying the public-sector capital formation rate by the ratio of government capital formation to government factor income (payments by the public sector to land, labor, and capital) as share of GDP.

[2] Population-weighted mean. Australia, Canada, and Italy are omitted from the gross public investment rate because data on public-sector investment are either unavailable or incomplete.

Sources: Increases in tax revenue computed from Organization for Economic Cooperation and Development, *Revenue Statistics of OECD Member Countries, 1965-1990* (Paris: OECD,1991), Table 4, p. 74; Gross public- and private-sector investment computed from United Nations, *National Accounts Statistics: Main Aggregates and Detailed Tables, 1988,* Parts I and II (New York: United Nations, 1990).

and experienced the highest rate of public-sector capital formation. The opposite was the case for the United States. The OECD countries occupied an intermediate position with regard to both variables.

There is also a statistically significant relationship between the increase in the share of the GDP collected in non-social-security taxation and the adjusted rate of public-sector investment for the nine countries for which data are available. These impressive results are displayed in Table 5.[12] The pattern laid out is consistent with the hypothesis that increasing the tax share allowed governments to encourage productivity growth by engaging in their own capital formation.

Table 5
Increase in Tax Revenues, Excluding Social Security, as a Percentage of Gross Domestic Product, 1975–89, and Adjusted Public-Sector Investment Rate, 1979–88

	Increase in Taxes, Excluding Social Security, as a Percentage of GDP	Public-Sector Investment Rate
Japan	7.2	3.90
France	2.7	0.64
Australia	2.5	1.13
Sweden	6.3	0.56
United Kingdom	0.7	0.26
Belgium	0.6	0.39
Germany	0.5	0.74
Netherlands	0.3	0.64
United States	-0.6	0.22

$r = 0.7104$
$r^2 = 0.5047$

Sources: Increase in tax revenue computed from Organization for Economic Cooperation and Development, Revenue Statistics of OECD Member Countries, 1965-1990 (Paris: OECD, 1991), Table 4, p. 74; Public-sector investment rate compiled from United Nations, National Accounts Statistics: Main Aggregates and Detailed Tables, 1988, Parts I and II (New York: United Nations, 1990).

This finding should not be taken to indicate that causality flowed only in one direction. If a growing public sector contributed to productivity growth, this does not mean that the converse was invalid. What might be called a virtuous circle may play out in this situation: productivity growth may stimulate further productivity growth by making it relatively easy to increase the size of the public sector. The positive contribution the public sector can make toward increasing the productivity of an economy, however, has only recently begun to receive the attention it deserves. Indeed, the contrary argument is much more frequently voiced; there is a widespread belief that an enhanced public sector harms productivity because rising taxes constrain private investment. This is clearly incorrect. The Japanese not only had the highest public-sector investment rate in Figure 3, but its private-sector investment rate also exceeded that of the others. Similarly, capital formation in the United States was the lowest both in the public and private sectors.[13] The data presented here do not contradict the notion that increased productivity facilitates tax collection; but they lend weight to the argument that increased tax collection has a role to play in wealth creation.

Tax Aversion as a Particularly American Trait

The United States certainly does not suffer from overtaxation. In 1989, the last year for which complete data are available, the tax burden in this country was lower than in either Japan or the other OECD countries (see Table 1). Even more important, over the period 1970 to 1989 the non-Social Security tax burden in this country actually declined (see Table 2). This decline seems to be associated with the limited amount of public-sector investment in the United States—only 28.6 percent of the equivalent for Japan and 57.5 percent of the figure for the OECD countries. It seems possible that the low tax burden in this country, by depriving the economy of public-sector investment, seriously undermines our efforts to achieve high levels of productivity.

Tax Structure and Revenue Raising in Industrial Countries

The reasons for the relative shortfall in tax revenue in the United States lend themselves to comparative analysis. A comparison of this country's public sector with those in Japan and the OECD nations must take into consideration the kind of taxes that are relied upon; the degree of progressivity of each country's income tax; and the pattern of expenditures across countries. By exploring the ways in which the United States differs from Japan and the OECD countries in revenue collection and the spending of public resources, the following section of this paper will seek insight into why the United States undertaxes itself.

The tax structures in the United States on the one hand and in Japan and the other OECD countries on the other hand differ in several respects. These differences become dramatically clear in studying Table 6, which groups governmental revenue by its tax source. The first and most surprising difference is Japan's relatively heavy reliance on the corporate income tax. More than one-fifth of government revenue in Japan comes from this source, compared to less than one-tenth in the United States and the OECD countries. The table also reveals that the United States depends more heavily than the others on the personal income and property taxes. Almost one-half (46.3 per cent) of taxes collected in this country comes from these two sources; the corresponding percentages are 33.7 in Japan and

Table 6
Type of Tax as Percentage of
Total Tax Revenue, 1970–89

	United States	Japan	OECD[1]
Personal Income	35.3	23.9	26.6
Corporate Income	9.1	22.8	7.5
Property	11.0	9.8	5.8
Goods and Services	17.4	15.2	29.1
Social Security[2]	27.1	28.1	30.5

[1] Population-weighted mean for Australia, Austria, Belgium, Canada, Denmark, France, Germany, Italy, Netherlands, Norway, Sweden, United Kingdom.

[2] Data for Australia are not available.

Source: Calculated from Organization for Economic Cooperation and Development, Revenue Statistics of OECD Member Countries, 1965-1990 (Paris: OECD, 1991), Table 11, p. 77; Table 13, p. 78; Table 23, p. 83; Table 25, p. 84; and Table 15, p. 79.

32.4 in the OECD group. Finally, the table makes apparent that the OECD relies much more heavily than the United States or Japanese governments on taxation of goods and services. Taxes on goods and services account for almost 30 percent of government tax revenues in the OECD, well above the 17.4 percent recorded by the United States and 15.2 percent by Japan. To summarize, this table indicates that the United States 1) relies more heavily on personal income and property taxes than both of the others, 2) employs the corporate income tax to a lesser extent than the Japanese, and 3) depends on taxes on goods and services less than the OECD.

PROGRESSIVITY AND POPULAR SUPPORT

In light of the heavy reliance on the income and property taxes in the United States, it is of considerable interest that polls consistently suggest that these are the two most unpopular taxes in the country. Data on public attitudes concerning the fairness of various taxes are provided in Tables 7 and 8. These figures reveal the depth of Americans' distaste for the nation's most significant taxes. The results were not altered when (after 1988) the Social Security tax was added to the list that respondents were requested to consider. The most straightforward interpretation of these findings is that the hostility to income and property taxes simply reflects the government's dependence on them. There may, however, be more to it than that. There are reasons to believe that, over and above the hostility generated by their extensive use, these taxes, at least as presently structured in the United States, might be considered unfair by the populace even at lower levels of taxation than prevail at present.

In the first place the income tax in the United States is less progressive than in either Japan or various OECD countries. Employing data marshaled by the late Joseph A. Pechman, Table 9 constructs an index of tax progressivity for the United States, Japan, and nine of the OECD countries that were considered earlier. This index of progressivity is derived by subtracting the effective tax rate for married couples with two children earning the income equivalent of an average production worker's salary from the effective tax rate for similar households earning ten times that income level.[14] The larger the number—the greater the difference in the effective tax rates between the two groups—the greater the degree of progressivity.

As indicated in the table, the index of tax progressivity for the United States is lower than either Japan's or the mean for the OECD countries. In

Table 7
Responses to the Question
"Which Do You Think Is the Worst Tax—That Is, the Least Fair"
(Percent)

	Federal Income	State Income	State Sales	Local Property	Don't Know
1991	26	12	19	30	14
1990	NA	NA	NA	NA	NA
1989	27	10	18	32	13
1988	33	10	18	28	11
1987	30	12	21	24	13
1986	37	8	17	28	10
1985	38	10	16	24	12
1984	36	10	15	29	10
1983	35	11	13	26	15
1982	36	11	14	30	9
1981	36	9	14	33	9
1980	36	10	19	25	10
1979	37	8	15	27	13
1978	30	11	18	32	10
1977	28	11	17	33	11
1976	NA	NA	NA	NA	NA
1975	28	11	23	29	10
1974	30	10	20	28	14
1973	30	10	20	31	11
1972	19	13	13	45	11
20-Year Average	32	10	16	30	11

Source: Advisory Commission on Intergovernmental Relations, Changing Public Attitudes on Governments and Taxes, 1991, S-20, Washington, D.C., 1991, Table 1, p. 4.

Table 8
Responses to the Question
"Which Do You Think Is the Worst Tax—That Is, the Least Fair, Including Social Security Taxes" (Percent)

	Federal Income	Social Security	State Income	State Sales	Local Property	Don't Know
1990	26	15	10	12	28	9
1989	21	18	9	14	28	10
1988	26	17	9	15	24	9

Source: Advisory Commission on Intergovernmental Relations, *Changing Public Attitudes on Governments and Taxes, 1990*, S-19, Washington, D.C., 1991, Table 2, p. 4.

fact, income taxation in the United States ranks as the least progressive of all of the eleven countries included in the Pechman study. The United States' low score on the index can largely be accounted for by the relatively high rate at which average-income households are taxed. The tax rate for such families in the United States is 7.3 percent, compared to just 0.3 percent in Japan. In contrast, high-income households are taxed at comparable rates in Japan and the United States. The nine OECD countries also tax average-income households less than does the United States, but in addition they tax high-income households more.[15]

The data in Table 9 support the hypothesis that progressivity in the income tax encourages relatively high tax burdens. There is a statistically significant relationship between the index of income tax progressivity for 1989 and the share of the gross domestic product paid as taxes in 1988: the higher the index of progressivity, the higher are tax revenues as a percentage of gross domestic product. It would seem to be safe to conclude that in Western capitalist democracies, the electorate supports high levels of taxation when the income tax is progressive. Since the income tax in the United States is less progressive than elsewhere, it may be the case that this characteristic contributes to the electorate's reluctance in this country to support a relatively high tax burden.

Table 9
Index of Effective Income Tax Progressivity for Nine OECD Countries, Japan, and the United States, 1989

Country	(1) Effective Tax Rate for Average-Income Production Workers	(2) Effective Tax Rate for High-Income Production Workers	(2)-(1)	Tax/ GDP (1988)
United States	7.3	32.8	25.5	29.8
Japan	0.3	31.9	31.6	31.3
Australia	14.3	43.7	29.4	30.8
Canada	6.4	38.4	32.0	34.0
Denmark	28.7	61.6	32.9	52.1
France	-17.2	30.7	47.9	44.4
Germany	5.7	44.1	38.4	37.4
Italy	1.9	31.9	30.0	37.1
Netherlands	-1.4	47.9	49.3	48.2
Sweden	20.3	62.4	42.1	55.3
United Kingdom	2.2	31.3	29.1	37.3
Mean OECD*	1.1	37.4	36.3	39.2

* Population-weighted mean.

Correlation between index of progressivity and tax/GDP:
$r = 0.6698$, significant at the 0.05 confidence level.
$r^2 = 0.4486$

Source: Joseph A. Pechman, "Tax Treatment of Families in Modern Industrial Countries: The Role of the NIT," *Focus* 12, no. 3 (Spring 1990), Table 2, p. 34; U.S. Department of Commerce, Bureau of the Census, "Taxes as Percentage of Gross Domestic Product," *Statistical Abstract of the United States, 1991* (Washington, D.C.: Government Printing Office, 1991), Table 1457, p. 846.

The evidence concerning the public's attitude toward tax progressivity in the United States generally is supportive of this hypothesis. Kevin Phillips reports that the American people strongly favor progressive taxes. He cites a 1987 National Opinion Research Center (NORC) poll, which found that 59 percent of Americans believed that the wealthy were insufficiently taxed. Phillips cites a staff member of NORC as saying that "the soaking-the-rich approach [to raising government revenues] has been quite popular among Americans since the 1930s."[16] Even Benjamin Page and Robert Shapiro, who believe that "the American public has not expressed much support for the kind of progressive taxation that would be required to redistribute incomes substantially," nonetheless concede that polls have revealed that most Americans believe that the rich should pay more.[17]

Estimation of the progressivity of the other tax upon which the United States relies extensively, the property tax, is fraught with conceptual and measurement problems. It is possible, however, to set up a cross-country examination of the relationship between reliance on the property tax and the tax/GDP ratio. These results are presented in Table 10. There is a statistically significant inverse relationship between the importance of the property tax as a source of revenue and the share of GDP represented by taxation. Where countries depend heavily on the property tax, their overall tax intake tends to be relatively small. This negative correlation is considerably strengthened when one outlier, Italy, is dropped from the sample of countries. Following that omission, 54 percent of the variance in relative tax burdens is explained by the differences in the percentage contribution of property taxes to total revenue.

It appears that the more a country relies on the property tax, the more difficult it is to tax at all. Taxpayers typically are confronted with one or two large bills for property tax each year. More conscious of their yearly liability for property tax than they are of most other taxes, taxpayers seem to react to the burden of the financial setback with an aversion to taxes in any form. The hostility to taxation triggered by the income tax, in contrast, seems to be less intense (refer back to Table 7). A sensible conjecture is that the antitax sentiment resulting from the income tax may be mitigated by its progressivity; in this respect it is unlike (except in rare circumstances) the property tax. Taxes on goods and services, extensively used in other OECD countries (particularly in the European Community, with its value-added tax) but not in Japan or the United States, apparently generate even less

Table 10
Property Taxation as a
Percentage of All Tax Revenues
for Fourteen Countries, 1989

Country	Property Tax as Percentage of All Tax Revenues	Taxation (overall)/ GDP
United States	10.3	29.8
Australia	8.8	30.8
Japan	10.2	31.3
Canada	8.8	34.0
Italy	2.3	37.1
United Kingdom	12.6	37.3
Germany	3.1	37.4
Austria	2.7	41.9
France	5.0	44.4
Belgium	2.7	45.1
Norway	2.9	46.9
Netherlands	3.8	48.2
Denmark	4.3	52.1
Sweden	3.3	55.3

$r = -0.6628$
$r^2 = -0.4393$

Source: Organization for Economic Cooperation and Development, Revenue Statistics of OECD Member Countries, 1965–1990 (Paris: OECD, 1991), Table 23, p. 83.

anger than the income tax. The relatively benign reaction to it probably is rooted in the inconspicuousness of the tax, hidden as it is in the prices of commodities.

It may therefore be an oversimplification to argue that people in the United States are hostile to the income tax and property tax because those are the heaviest taxes they pay. In the case of the property tax, people may be reacting to the lump-sum bill they confront; this may comport with the behavior of the public in other countries. The income tax here may be regarded unfavorably at least in part because it is thought of as insufficiently progressive. Certainly polling data and the correlation between progressivity and high tax/GDP ratios makes such a hypothesis appear plausible. If these speculations are valid, the pattern of taxation in the United States may explain at least part of the aversion to taxes in this country. It may be that our reliance on the property tax and a relatively unprogressive income tax is a source of the difficulty.

GOVERNMENT SPENDING AND POPULAR SUPPORT

This paper has discussed at length the means governments use to raise revenue; the other side of the ledger—how they spend it—also demands consideration. Figure 4 makes clear that none of the other countries under consideration approach Japan's public-sector investment rate. While Japan's adjusted gross public-sector investment rate is close to 4 percent of gross domestic product, only one other country, Australia, exceeds 1 percent of GDP. The United States ranks at the bottom of this list with an adjusted gross public-sector investment rate of 0.22 percent. The population-weighted investment mean rate of 0.59 percent for the other OECD countries for which data are available places them closer to the United States than to Japan.

Tables 11 and 12 rank public-sector spending by function using the United Nations classification system. The single biggest gap that shows up in these comparisons is the difference in defense expenditures between the United States and the other industrialized nations. In the 1980s, the United States spent more than 6 percent of its gross domestic product on military expenditures, approximately twice the level of the OECD group and more than six times that of Japan. The United States also spent relatively more than Japan and about the same as the OECD countries on education, though the rate of U.S. spending in this category declined 6.24 percent between the

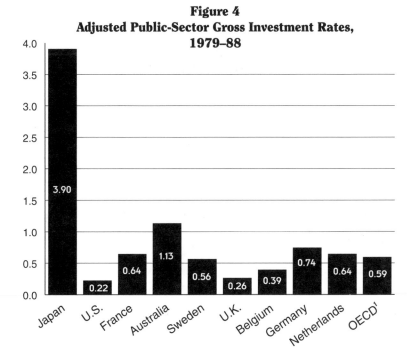

Figure 4
Adjusted Public-Sector Gross Investment Rates,
1979–88

¹ Population-weighted mean for France, Australia, Sweden, United Kingdom, Belgium, Germany, and Netherlands.

Source: United Nations, *National Accounts Statistics: Main Aggregates and Detailed Tables, 1988,* Parts I and II (New York: United Nations, 1990).

1970s and 1980s. Finally, the OECD countries spent more both on social welfare and health than either Japan or the United States. During the 1980s these two categories of public expenditure in the OECD nations accounted for 5.85 percent of the gross domestic product, compared to 1.53 percent in the United States and just 0.94 percent in Japan.

What these two tables seem to suggest is that a high proportion of the relatively small Japanese budget is spent on nondefense public-sector investment. In the United States, by contrast, a comparably small public sector is disproportionately devoted to defense spending. Japan puts a lower priority on educational expenditures than the rest, but it acted to close the gap with the United States, if not the OECD countries, in the 1980s, a period of relative decline in educational spending in the United

Table 11
Government Consumption
by Category as a Percentage of
Gross Domestic Product, 1970–79

Country	Defense	Education	Health	Social Welfare
Austria	1.08	3.29	3.86	0.94
Australia	2.53	4.26	2.59	0.39
Belgium	2.63	6.24	NA	1.02
France	NA	NA	NA	NA
Germany	2.96	3.66	5.35	1.52
Italy	1.92	4.11	3.32	0.90
Netherlands	3.09	6.29	NA	0.61
Norway	3.15	5.32	3.44	1.36
Sweden	3.22	5.45	5.96	3.33
United Kingdom	4.77	4.24	4.17	1.12
Mean OECD[1]	3.07	4.29	4.23	1.17
United States	5.87	4.81	1.07	0.52
Japan	0.83	3.47	0.39	0.43

[1] Population-weighted mean for Austria, Australia, Belgium, France, Germany, Italy, Netherlands, Norway, Sweden, and United Kingdom.

Source: Calculated from United Nations, *Yearbook of National Accounts Statistics, 1981* (New York: United Nations, 1983).

Table 12
Government Consumption
by Category as a Percentage
of Gross Domestic Product, 1980–88

Country	Defense	Education	Health	Social Welfare
Austria	1.19	4.10	4.48	3.45
Australia	2.42	4.36	3.17	0.63
Belgium	2.49	6.40	NA	1.24
France[1]	3.17	5.02	3.18	1.57
Germany	2.75	4.01	5.95	2.01
Italy	1.92	4.65	3.15	0.70
Netherlands	3.00	5.50	NA	0.76
Norway	3.01	5.05	4.44	1.76
Sweden	2.78	5.68	7.00	4.85
United Kingdom	4.98	4.17	4.83	1.44
Mean OECD[2]	3.05	4.60	4.34	1.51
United States	6.18	4.51	0.91	0.62
Japan	0.91	3.66	0.40	0.54

[1] 1983–86 only.

[2] Population-weighted mean for Austria, Australia, Belgium, France, Germany, Italy, Netherlands, Norway, Sweden, and United Kingdom.

Source: Calculated from United Nations, *National Accounts Statistics, Main Aggregates and Detailed Tables, 1988,* Parts I and II (New York: United Nations, 1990).

States. The OECD nations, with relatively higher tax burdens than either Japan or the United States, devote a far higher share of their output to public-sector health and social welfare expenditures, though almost all the countries concerned exhibited an expansion of the social service sector during the 1980s.

This analysis permits speculation that not only the means of taxation but the way tax revenues are expended in the United States plays at least some role in fostering tax aversion. The low level of U.S. public investment means that, in contrast to Japan and other OECD countries, government spending is not linked in the public mind to the sources of productivity growth and increasing economic well-being. The belief that taxation can directly contribute to economic well-being would be encouraged if people observed their government investing in productivity-raising infrastructure. Conversely, the very heavy defense burden that the citizens of the United States support may reinforce the belief that taxes are swallowed by a centralized bureaucracy, the benefits of which are never to be seen. The defense budget has a direct impact on a relatively small proportion of the population and labor force, though, of course, its indirect effect is more widespread. If it is the case that people react most favorably when they can directly observe the benefits of taxation, as in highway construction or new communications satellites, then defense spending may represent a too narrowly focused category of spending, with too little impact on the everyday lives of the people, to build a case for greater government expenditure.

Page and Shapiro generally agree with the view that the way public money is spent in the United States contributes to the hostility toward taxation. They report that, according to a CBS/*New York Times* poll, "majorities of the public were, in fact, willing to cut programs such as foreign aid and military spending. . . . The truth of the matter seems to be that most people oppose large parts of the federal budget that have been identified as 'wasteful'—most important, in the 1980s and 1990s, military spending." They expand on this point:

> People oppose general tax rises that would be spent on things they don't want. Again and again survey questions . . . report that majorities of Americans say they are willing to pay more taxes for specific purposes like medical care and research, Social Security, education, and the environment.[18]

In general, then, it appears that the way we tax and spend public revenues in this country contributes to the broad unpopularity and low level of taxation found in the United States. On one side, the property tax seems to be unpopular everywhere, and our income tax may not be sufficiently progressive to generate political support. Furthermore, the United States only employs taxes on goods and services to a limited extent, even though they do not trigger the hostility encountered by other forms of taxation. On the other side, our pattern of public-sector expenditures are not of a character that mobilizes a supporting constituency; our governments spend inadequately on projects that demonstrably and explicitly contribute to the economic well-being of the public. If these hypotheses are valid, tax aversion in the United States may be rooted more in public policy than in an ubiquitous antistate animus.

PATTERNS OF PUBLIC FINANCE AND INVESTMENT

During the 1970s and 1980s dramatic changes occurred both in the financing of public-sector expenditures and in the pattern of investment carried out by the U.S. government. First, there was a decline in traditional sources of government revenue (that is, taxes). Second, tax revenues suffered a relative decline as a percentage of government expenditures.

THE DIMINISHING IMPORTANCE
OF TAXATION FOR REVENUE

Table 13 provides data on the revenue sources for all levels of government between 1970 and 1988. The decline in the importance of taxation is shown on the first line. Tax revenue in proportion to government revenue fell from 82.4 percent in 1970 to 74.8 percent in 1988. The counterpart of this decline was the growth that occurred in the relative importance of nontax revenues for financing the budget, shown on the last line of the table.

The fall in the importance of traditional taxation was only partially offset by increases in insurance trust funds. Thus, as indicated in Table 13, the relative importance of general taxes fell from 69.8 percent in 1970 to 56.2 percent in 1988. Of the major sources of tax revenue, the largest relative decline was in the corporate income tax and the least significant was in individual income taxes.

Table 13
Percentage Distribution of Government
Revenue by Source,
Selected Years, 1970–88*

	1970	1980	1988
Total Tax Revenue	82.4	78.2	74.8
Property	10.2	7.3	7.4
Individual Income	30.3	30.7	27.6
Corporate Income	11.0	8.4	6.6
Sales and Gross Receipts	14.6	12.0	11.8
Motor Vehicle and Operator Licenses	0.9	0.6	0.6
Death and Gift	1.4	0.9	0.6
All Other General	1.5	1.7	1.6
General Taxes	69.8	61.6	56.2
Insurance Trust Funds	12.6	16.6	18.7
Nontax Revenues, Total	17.6	21.8	25.1

* Federal, state, and local government included.

Source: Paul G. Merski et al., Facts and Figures on Government Finance, 1991 (Baltimore: Johns Hopkins University Press, 1991), Table A13, p. 15.

In principle, a gap between tax revenues and government expenditures can be made up by increasing charges and fees for services provided, by borrowing, and, where possible, through intergovernmental transfers. At the federal level, however current charges and fees did not increase in relative importance. As a result, all of the shortfall in taxation was made up by increased governmental borrowing. By the middle of the 1980s one-fifth of federal expenditures were financed through borrowing, and the percentage declined only slightly by the end of the decade.

All of the relative decline in the importance of taxation as revenue occurred at the federal level (Table 14). Whereas taxes as a percentage of expenditures declined from 56.9 to 46.3 percent for the federal government, at the state and local level the percentage actually increased, from 51.4 to 52.7 percent. The problem at the state and local level was that during the 1980s a major source of revenue, intergovernmental transfers from the federal government, declined from 19.1 percent of expenditures to 14.3 percent (Table 14) reversing the pattern of the 1970s. The increase in the relative importance of taxes at the state and local level was insufficient to make up for the loss. As a result, state and local governments resorted increasingly to current charges for services; the proportion of expenditures funded in this way rose from 17.6 percent in 1980 to 21.0 percent in 1988.

CHANGES IN THE COMPOSITION OF CAPITAL SPENDING

While these adjustments in government finances were taking place, changes were also were occurring in the magnitude and pattern of public investment in this country (see Table 15). Public-sector investment represented 3.31 percent of the gross domestic product in 1970. By 1985 that figure had declined to 2.30 percent. In fact, the recent low point in public-sector investment occurred in 1984, when its share of GDP stood at 2.18 percent. A slight recovery occurred by 1988, but by this time, the rate of public investment was only about three-quarters of the comparable 1970 figure.

Investment rates in three of the five largest components of public-sector investment—education, highways, and housing—followed the general pattern of precipitous declines between 1970 and 1985, followed by a slight recovery in the years afterward. The highway investment rate dropped by 45 percent between 1970 and 1985, recovering about 6 percent of that loss in the following three years. Education investment fell by 56 percent between 1970 and 1985, also achieving a small recovery by 1988. Housing followed a similar pattern of decline until 1980 and then recovery, though in this instance the recovery was large enough that capital expenditures on housing by government in 1988 represented, proportionally to GDP, 86 percent of their 1970 level. Investment in natural resources, however, fell continuously, reaching a new low in 1988 of only 44 percent relative to 1970. Of the largest sectors of public investment, only utilities recorded an increase in the rate of investment. Notwithstanding a drop in the utility investment rate in the years subsequent to its peak in 1980, public-sector investment in utilities in 1988 stood at a level 25 percent higher than in 1970.

Table 14
Sources of Government Expenditures by
Level of Government, 1980–1988
(Percentage of Total Expenditures)

	All[1]	Federal	State and Local
Taxation			
1980	59.9	56.9	51.4
1985	50.9	44.0	53.2
1988	52.0	46.3	52.7
Current Charges and Miscellaneous			
1980	14.8	10.9	17.6
1985	15.6	10.1	21.6
1988	15.7	10.5	21.0
Intergovernmental Transfers			
1980	-	-	19.1
1985	-	-	16.1
1988	-	-	14.3
Budgetary Deficit/Surplus			
1980	-2.8	-8.4	+4.1
1985	-10.2	-21.8	+9.4
1988	-7.5	-16.7	+7.0

[1] Excludes duplicative transactions among levels of government.

Source: U.S. Department of Commerce, Bureau of the Census, Statistical Abstract of the United States, 1991 (Washington, D.C.: Government Printing Office, 1991), Table 465, p. 279.

Table 15
Nondefense-related Public-Sector Investment by Function at All Levels of Government, as a Percentage of Gross Domestic Product, Selected Years, 1970–1988

	1970	1975	1980	1985	1988
Education	0.75	0.62	0.40	0.33	0.38
Highways	1.07	0.86	0.71	0.59	0.65
Health and Hospitals	0.09	0.13	0.12	0.09	0.10
Natural Resources	0.25	0.29	0.19	0.14	0.11
Housing*	0.21	0.18	0.09	0.13	0.18
Air Transport	0.09	0.08	0.06	0.07	0.07
Water Transport	0.05	0.04	0.06	0.03	0.03
Sewerage	0.14	0.23	0.23	0.15	0.17
Parks and Recreation	0.07	0.08	0.07	0.05	0.06
Utilities	0.24	0.31	0.37	0.33	0.30
Other	0.35	0.47	0.33	0.37	0.47
Total	3.31	3.29	2.63	2.30	2.51

*
Includes community development .

Sources: For figures on public-sector investment, see U.S. Department of Commerce, Bureau of the Census, Statistical Abstract of the United States, 1991 (Washington, D.C.: Government Printing Office,1991), Table 467, p. 281; for figures on gross domestic product, see Economic Report of the President, 1992 (Washington, D.C.: Government Printing Office, 1992), Table B-1, p. 298.

WHAT IS RESPONSIBLE FOR THE
DECLINE IN PUBLIC INVESTMENT?

The question that arises in this context is what, if any, relationship exists between the relative fall in the importance of taxation as a means to support government expenditures at all levels and the decline in public-sector investment. To investigate this relationship, it is necessary to compare the experience of the federal government on the one hand and state and local governments on the other. Figure 5 indicates that between 1980 and 1988 federal taxes as a percentage of GDP fell, while state and local taxes increased their share slightly. During these same years, however, capital investment at the federal level as a percentage of GDP increased while investment at the state and local level declined. This pattern seems to suggest that what is happening to taxes does not dictate public-sector investment.

Figure 5

**Taxes
as a Percentage of GDP
by Level of Government**

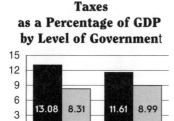

**Total Resource Availability[1]
as a Percentage of GDP
by Level of Government**

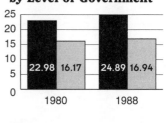

■ Federal   ▢ State and Local

**Nondefense Capital
Outlays as a Percentage
of GDP by Level of Government**

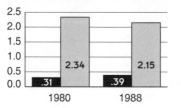

[1] Total resource availability is equal to the total expenditure of that level of government divided by GDP for the year examined.

Source: Computed from U.S. Department of Commerce, Bureau of the Census, *Statistical Abstract of the United States, 1991* (Washington, D.C.: Government Printing Office, 1991), Table 465, p. 279; Table 467, p. 281; and Table 699, p. 432.

Yet, as has been seen, taxes are not the only source of public revenue; indeed, they are a decreasing fraction of the total revenues received by governments at all levels. The second panel of Figure 5 provides information concerning all sources of revenue, including governmental deficits and surpluses. This statistic, more than the tax revenue statistic alone, provides insight into the real resource availability that confronted governmental officials trying to determine their expenditure decisions. Obviously the pattern is very different from the one that applies to tax revenues alone. When all other nontax resources were combined with tax revenues, the federal government's claim on the GDP increased by 8.3 percent (from 22.98 to 24.89 percentage points), accompanied by an increase in its investment/GDP ratio from 0.31 to 0.39 percent. At the same time, the claim made by state and local government on GDP increased by only 4.8 percent (from 16.17 to 16.94 percentage points), an increase that was associated with an 8.1 percent falloff in state and local capital spending. This decrease may be the consequence of increasing pressures to reallocate spending away from capital projects toward other areas in the face of tight budgets caused in part by the stagnating resource base available to many state and local governments.

If public investment is considered a source of productivity growth, these patterns suggest a serious problem in the United States. The problem results from two peculiarities present in this country. The first is that public investment overwhelmingly occurs at the state and local level. As Figure 5 shows, nondefense public investment at the state and local level, even in 1988, was 5.5 times what the federal government contributed. The second is that the federal government alone enjoys virtually unlimited access to credit. When the federal government borrows, its access to credit is never an issue because of the Federal Reserve's ability to monetize its debt. That is not the case with regard to other units of government, however. For states, counties, and towns, an increase in the need to borrow typically results in a downgrading in the bond rating agencies' evaluation of governmental creditworthiness, with the result either that a locality's borrowing becomes more expensive or, in the most extreme case, it is shut out of the market entirely.

The problem is that the level of government that is best able to raise money from both tax and nontax sources, the federal, is a minor participant, relatively speaking, in public investment. State and local governments, which undertake most public-sector investment, are constrained by their inability to borrow freely. This constraint is responsible for the decline in public investment as a percentage of the GDP in this country during the 1980s.

The international cross-sectional analysis done earlier found that the countries where tax revenues grew the most were the ones in which public-sector investment and productivity increased most substantially. The conclusion follows that causality flowed from taxation to investment and productivity growth as well as vice versa. The same general causal flow seems to be present in the United States as elsewhere, but there is an important additional level of complexity here that militates against public investment. Because of resource constraints, state and local governments are under pressure to reduce their level of capital outlays. The federal government, by contrast, still is able to raise the revenue it requires but plays a relatively small role in undertaking public investment. The problem is institutionalized in our federal system.

BETTER LIVING THROUGH IMPROVEMENTS
IN INFRASTRUCTURE AND EDUCATION

There are two ways in which public spending can lead to productivity growth. It can increase the stock of public capital, thereby facilitating production. No less important, the educational system represents an investment in human capital and thereby advances the potential productivity of the economy in the future. Concerning the first method of investment, David Alan Aschauer, the pioneer in the field, argues that spending on infrastructure contributes to productivity because such public amenities as highways and airports directly facilitate private production. In addition, he says, public capital and private factors of production may be complementary. The increase in private production consequent to an improvement in infrastructure may itself induce the use of new resources and improved methods of production.[19]

INFRASTRUCTURE AND PRODUCTIVITY

Two kinds of important evidence have been produced to support the assertion that public investment is a critical source of productivity growth. Aschauer has generated a time series for the United States that explicitly includes public capital as an input into the production function. His definition takes into account what he calls "core infrastructure": streets and highways, mass transit, airport, water, and sewerage systems, and electrical and gas facilities. He reports a significant and strong positive association between such public investment and both labor productivity and total factor productivity.[20]

In addition, both Aschauer and Alicia H. Munnell have tested this public investment thesis using interregional data. Aschauer examines the relationship between public investment and productivity across the Group of Seven countries, and Munnell does so for states within the United States. In both cases, significant positive relationships were found between the stock of public capital and productivity. Munnell's effort has commanded considerable professional respect because in undertaking her production-function analysis she was required to construct new estimates of public capital created by each state. Furthermore, Munnell reports that in disaggregating her results she found that water and sewerage systems, followed by highways, had the largest impact on productivity.[21]

Aschauer's and Munnell's findings have triggered a lively controversy. Henry J. Aaron, though conceding that "Aschauer has had a valuable insight," nonetheless believes that he "has greatly exaggerated its quantitative importance."[22] Similarly, Charles R. Hulten, in discussing a paper by Munnell, finds no great surprise in her position that public investment contributes to productivity growth. Instead, he emphasizes that the elasticity of supply for public capital, in her estimates, is considerably lower than that for private capital.[23]

What is significant about these and other reactions is that virtually no one has argued the contrary claim, that public capital makes no contribution to productivity growth. Aschauer's estimates, in particular, have been criticized for being too high. But even his most stringent critics acknowledge that he has made a contribution to the discussion of the sources of the productivity problem in this country. There now seems to be a consensus among economists that public capital is of importance in achieving greater efficiency of production.

EDUCATION AND PRODUCTIVITY

Educational advances within a population are widely viewed as essential before improvements in productive efficiency can be achieved. As a recent World Bank publication has stated, "Because knowledge is an increasingly important and unique factor of production, it has to be treated explicitly as a separate factor of production, not as a residual of our ignorance."[24] In the United States, where almost 90 percent of elementary and secondary students attended public schools in 1989, it is evident that the performance of the public education system is an important source of the human capital that contributes to technological and productivity advances.[25]

The quality of education and its implications for the economy have been a concern since a decline in standardized test scores was observed in the late 1960s. In general this decline, illustrated by SAT and ACT test scores in Figure 6, continued until about 1980, when a slow reversal took hold. Evidence of inadequate educational performance is reinforced when international test scores are compared.This comparison (indicated in Table 16) makes it clear that the United States in 1970 ranked at or near the bottom in mathematics and science tests, two areas that are critical for future technological advances.[26] More recent international math test scores,

Figure 6
Scholastic Aptitude Test (SAT) Math Scores and
American College Testing (ACT) Program Math Scores,
Selected Years, 1967–89

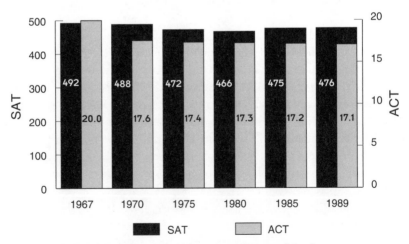

Source: U.S. Department of Commerce, Bureau of the Census, Statistical Abstract of the United States, 1991 (Washington, D.C.: Government Printing Office, 1991), Tables 253 and 254, p. 154.

Table 16
Average Test Scores in Mathematics and
Science for Secondary Students, 1970

	Percentage of Answers Correct	
	Math	Science
Japan	45.5	NA
France	48.8	30.5
United Kingdom	51.0	38.5
Sweden	39.6	32.0
Netherlands	46.2	38.8
Germany	41.7	44.8
Europe	45.5	36.9
Austria	NA	NA
United States	20.0	22.8

Source: Louis Ferleger and Jay R. Mandle, "Co-signs and Derivations of America's Two-Score Decline: Poor Math Skills, Poor Productivity Growth," *Challenge* 35, no. 3 (May/June 1992), Table 2, p. 49.

displayed in Tables 17 and 18, suggest that this country is still substantially lagging behind other OECD countries.

In a recent article, John H. Bishop considers the impact of the test score decline on productivity.[27] He does so by using the results of the Iowa Test of Educational Development as the basis for constructing a measure of general intellectual achievement (GIA). This, in turn, is examined together with wage data to consider its effect on labor productivity. Bishop's GIA measure starts to fall around 1967, a downward trend without precedent in the historical experience of the United States. This decline, however, did not affect children in grades one through three. Bishop notes: "The decline appears to have been caused by something that happened to children after third grade." He is uncertain about the causes of the fall in test scores. He writes that "the decline was larger for whites than for minorities and larger in the suburbs than in central city high schools with student bodies from

Table 17
Average Percentage of Correct Scores in Mathematics by Thirteen-Year-Olds, Selected Countries, 1990–91

Country	Average Percentage Correct
France	64.2
Italy[1]	64.0
Canada	62.0
England	60.6
IAEP[2]	58.3
United States	55.3

[1] Data for Emilia-Romagna, Italy.

[2] IAEP is the average score of the twenty participants in the study: Brazil, Canada, China, England, France, Hungary, Ireland, Israel, Italy, Jordan, South Korea, Mozambique, Portugal, Scotland, Slovenia, Soviet Union, Spain, Switzerland, Taiwan, United States. Four countries had lower scores than the United States: Brazil, Jordan, Mozambique, and Portugal.

Source: Archie E. Lapointe, Nancy A. Mead, and Janice M. Askew, *Learning Mathematics*, report prepared for the National Center of Educational Statistics, U.S. Department of Education and the National Science Foundation, February 1992, pp. 6, 10, 145.

disadvantaged backgrounds." Declines occurred in both private and public schools and affected the more able students as much as they did those who did not perform well in school (see Table 18).

Bishop estimates the effect of the decline of GIA on productivity for three groups: those who obtained twelve or fewer years of formal education, those with one to four years of college education, and those who entered graduate school. The major impact on the productivity of these groups was felt only after about 1980. By his estimates, which Bishop argues are conservative, the effect of the decline in the quality of the labor force as measured by test scores reduced the gross national product by 0.9 percent in 1980 and 1.9 percent in 1987. Furthermore, Bishop is at pains to point out that the consequences for the economy in all likelihood will remain dire as the relatively poorly educated workers age.

Table 18
Average Percentage of Correct Scores in Mathematics by Thirteen-Year-Olds, Selected Countries, by Percentile, 1990–91

	1st	5th	10th	90th	95th	99th
	Average Percentage Correct					
France	22.7	30.7	37.3	89.3	92.0	97.3
Italy	23.0	32.4	36.5	88.0	91.8	96.0
Canada	21.3	32.0	37.3	86.7	91.8	97.3
England	18.7	27.4	34.5	89.3	93.3	97.3
United States	17.3	24.0	29.3	82.7	90.7	97.3

Source: Archie E. Lapointe, Nancy A. Mead, and Janice M. Askew, *Learning Mathematics*, report prepared for the National Center of Educational Statistics, U.S. Department of Education and the National Science Foundation, February 1992, pp. 6, 10, 145.

CONTRARY OPINIONS

Thus, there is a strong argument to be made that the nation needs both to augment the stock of public capital and to improve the quality of education in order to advance aggregate productivity. Even those who accept such a position in principle, however, do not necessarily believe that now is the time to undertake substantial new expenditures in these areas. Edward M. Gramlich, in a lecture on national priorities for the year 1992, concedes that improvements in physical and human capital are required. He argues, however, for deferring most such undertakings until what he describes as "structural change" is accomplished in each area. Gramlich calls for a change in the pricing mechanism that governs the use of infrastructure. He notes, for example, that auto and truck drivers treat roads as free goods, and tolls are set in such a way that they encourage road decay. He points out that the same is true regarding "airports, landfill dumps and most other kinds of public capital." As a result, he concludes that (aside from some additional expenditures to aid impoverished cities) "any large-scale attack on the public investment problem should await more sensible microeconomic policies."

Gramlich develops a similar argument with respect to education. He concedes that both education and health care "are lagging badly." However, the decline in test scores occurred while per pupil expenditures were being augmented, raising the question of whether additional expenditures on schooling will make the nation's schools merely more expensive, rather than better. Again conceding that there are exceptions where new spending is required immediately, Gramlich maintains that "it seems premature to invest large-scale resources into public education without more assurance that whatever problems are holding back educational productivity are resolved."[28] In other words, reform is necessary before incremental resources are devoted to education so as to ensure that those resources are efficiently used.

Though there is merit in Gramlich's case, his argument would be more powerful if public-sector investment and education in recent years had been the recipients of substantially greater resources. He does in fact cite an increase in per pupil expenditures during these years to bolster his case. But when investment in public primary and secondary education is calculated as a percentage of GDP, a downward trend is revealed (see Table 19). Indeed,

Table 19
Public Elementary and Secondary Education Capital Outlays and Public Nondefense Capital Expenditures as a Percentage of Gross Domestic Product, Selected Years, 1970–1988

	Public Education	Public Nondefense Capital
1970	0.46	3.31
1975	0.41	3.29
1980	0.27	2.63
1985	0.21	2.30
1988	0.24	2.51

Sources: For public education figures, see U.S. Department of Commerce, Bureau of the Census, *Statistical Abstract of the United States, 1991* (Washington, D.C.: Government Printing Office, 1991), Table 467, p. 281; and *Economic Report of the President, 1992* (Washington, D.C.: Government Printing Office, 1992), Table B-1, p. 298; for public nondefense capital figures, see Table 15.

the falloff in the importance of capital outlays in public education as a percentage of GDP is dramatic: between 1970 and 1988 the share of the national output devoted to investment in public education below the college level fell by 54.4 percent. Furthermore, per pupil public capital allocations also declined in real terms over these years, by 14.1 percent between 1970 and 1980 and by another 19.7 percent between 1980 and 1988.

As a result, by 1988 annual investment in education was almost one-third lower than it had been in 1970 (see Figure 7). Since public nondefense capital outlays as a percentage of GDP also fell, by 24.2 percent during these same years, it is not valid to argue that public investment and education have been allocated large increases in resources and that now is the time to retrench. It never is desirable to condone inefficiency, and to the extent that Gramlich points to the means by which a more productive use of resources can be attained, his proposals should be given urgent attention. But because both education and infrastructure have experienced a relative diminution in recent years, Gramlich's argument for a pause in the allocation of additional resources to them carries little force.

Figure 7
Public Capital Outlays for Elementary and Secondary Education per Person Aged 5–19, in 1982–84 Dollars: 1970, 1980, 1988

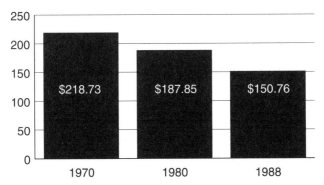

Source: Calculated from U.S. Department of Commerce, Bureau of the Census, *Statistical Abstract of the United States, 1991* (Washington, D.C.: Government Printing Office, 1991). For data on public capital outlays, see Table 467, p. 281; for data relating to population aged 5–19, see Table 13, p. 13; for consumer price index for personal and educational expenses, see Table 769, p. 477.

SHIFTING PRIORITIES IN INVESTMENT

In his discussion of the need for additional public investment, Aschauer makes the point that the pattern of such expenditures should not be unchanging over time. He writes, "We live in a dynamic economy which changes constantly in response to technological progress, foreign competitive pressures, and alterations in the demographic characteristics of the domestic workforce." In the future, he suggests, "infrastructure needs may well shift from surface to air transportation, from the transport of goods to that of ideas, and from a national to an international focus." Investment in airport and seaport facilities and telecommunications networking are areas that he suggests for near-term priority concern.[29]

John Bishop's analysis of the implications of the test score decline leads him also to a specific policy recommendation. He observes that "even if current efforts to improve the schools are successful, the test score decline will continue to depress productivity well into the 21st century." This is because the general intellectual achievement of those in the labor force now is at a lower level than previous cohorts with comparable years of school attendance. What this suggests to Bishop is the need to improve the GIA of adults. This might be accomplished "by attracting massive numbers of adults back into school, by expanding educational offerings on television and/or by inducing employers to provide general education to long-term employees."[30]

A policy aimed at investing in public and human capital must choose projects with care. In the cases of both education and infrastructure, expenditures must take into account the demands associated with advancing technology if they are to accomplish the aim of accelerating productivity growth. The effort to match infrastructure to the requirements of the new technology must build on the existing capital stock. Required also are programs to augment the previous training that the work force possesses, to keep labor quality from falling hopelessly behind the pace of innovation. Careful project-by-project attention must be devoted to the content of infrastructure investment and educational expenditures.

Adult and continuing education is one area that will require more attention than it has received in the past. Because economic growth requires the continuous application of new technological knowledge to production, the labor force must constantly augment its skills to be able to work efficiently with the new technology. Data that would permit a reliable comparison of adult education in the United States with the experience of comparable countries are unavailable. That the United States has a problem in this regard, however, is suggested by several recent studies. In a review of adult education and training programs carried out in the late 1970s in industrialized nations, Richard E. Peterson and coauthors remark that, in contrast to virtually all the other countries they studied, "it is fair to say that the U.S. government has no *comprehensive* adult education or occupation training policy."[31] In particular, the adult education experience in the United States seems to be at variance with Japan's. Ezra Vogel writes that "if any single factor explains Japanese [economic] success, it is the group directed quest for knowledge . . . . Adult education courses, offered by local communities, newspapers and department stores as well as universities, are extraordinarily popular."[32]

Awareness of the gap in adult education between the United States and the rest of the developed world is growing, and the subject has received renewed attention in recent years. Nonetheless, Nell P. Eurich notes that reforms "are late in coming. . . . much remedial training is required and it will continue to be needed at work force entry levels as well as in the ranks of older employees." She concludes that as yet, "opportunities [for adult education] are grossly inadequate."[33]

Just as important as continuously improving the skills of the adult labor force is the need to ensure that new workers, those leaving school for the first time, possess the skills to allow them to make a productive contribution to the economy. The changing composition of the student body nationwide, which will inevitably include more minority children and children raised in poverty, will create special difficulties for prospective employers in the future.[34] For, as Richard J. Murnane has written, "Increasingly, the students in American schools and the new entrants to the U.S. labor force will be individuals with characteristics that historically have been associated with low literacy and problem-solving skills." During a period of slow growth in the labor force, as the decade of the 1990s is likely to be, the skill level of these historically deprived groups, Murnane writes, "may have a significant impact on the productivity of the economy. . . ."[35] Thus it is entirely likely that the per pupil cost of education in the United States will have to rise in order to make certain that the economy is not hamstrung by an insufficient supply of adequately educated workers.

Installing an infrastructure appropriate to modern technology will be costly too. However, not a great deal of work or thought has been directed to this issue. The magazine *BusinessWeek* does consider the problem of infrastructure in its advocacy of an "industrial policy" for the United States. Citing Aschauer, *BusinessWeek* agrees that "government needs to refurbish decaying roads, harbors and bridges." But even more so than improvements to transportation, "building up a communications infrastructure that can support the information-intensive industries of the 1990s is critical." The editors of the magazine argue that a modern communications infrastructure is the present-day counterpart of the interstate highway network of a previous era. To date, insufficient public funds have been invested in promoting this project. The $400 million that has been budgeted for this project is "not enough, especially since many small companies won't get any benefits unless the government offers telephone companies and their competitors incentives to expand the data superhighway." [36]

FINDING THE FUNDS FOR CAPITAL SPENDING

It is not possible to provide even the crudest estimates of the cost of public and educational capital improvements that would be required to accelerate productivity growth in this country. But it seems reasonable to assume that the magnitude of the spending required for effective results would raise both public nondefense capital outlays and public educational expenditures at least to approximately their 1970 share of GDP. What this would mean is that in 1988, public investment would have stood at about 3.31 percent of GDP instead of 2.51 percent. In the case of education, outlays in 1988 would have represented about 0.75 percent of GDP, instead of 0.38 percent. However, as the data show, even as early as 1970 American students were already losing ground against their foreign counterparts. Therefore it would make good sense to earmark an additional 0.38 percent of GDP for educational expenditures, effectively tripling current outlays. If in 1988 public nondefense investment and educational spending were set at the 1970 rate, an additional 1.17 percent of the GDP would be spent. This represents roughly $60 billion. To put this additional $60 billion in perspective, consider that the federal deficit in 1988 stood at $155.1 billion, or 3.22 percent of GDP.

If all of the increased public investment in infrastructure and education were carried by the federal government, and if no additional taxes were imposed, the government deficit in 1988 would have increased by about 40 percent. To be sure, following the argument of Robert Eisner, if such expenditures were treated as an investment with a defered payoff, only depreciation should be charged to current outlays. Under that accounting procedure, the budget deficit would not have grown much at all.[37] Nonetheless, if new investment were to be financed through increased borrowing, the heightened demand for credit by the government would produce upward pressure on interest rates. Greater public investment might, under such circumstances, come at the expense of private investment. Such an outcome would be undesirable precisely because accelerating productivity growth in the economy requires high levels of both public and private investment.

An alternative way of finding the money for new public investment would be to reallocate budget expenditures. The ending of the cold war seems opportune in this respect. The reduced need for military preparedness might free sufficient resources from the defense budget to finance additional public investment. However, Gramlich has estimated that "the likely peace dividend appears to be much smaller than is commonly supposed." He points out that Congress and the president in their 1990 budget agreement reduced defense spending from 5.5 percent of GDP to about 4.3 percent. Unfortunately, the 1.2 percent of GDP taken from defense has already been spoken for in the anticipated extra government spending that formed part of the accord, spending that did not include major breakthroughs in nondefense public capital outlays or educational resources. Any hope for reallocating the federal budget in favor of investment would have to come from a more dramatic decline in military spending than has taken place so far.

Gramlich cites a Congressional Budget Office (CBO) study that analyzes the effect of an additional defense expenditure decline of 0.5 percent of GDP on top of the 1.2 percent figure in the 1990 agreement.[38] Such an additional decline in defense spending would be desirable as a means of increasing public investment. Even this, however, would be insufficient, providing at best only about 36 percent of the funds that would be necessary to achieve the proposed targets. With the ending of the cold war it is obvious that reduced defense spending is on the agenda; the only question is one of magnitude. The deeper political problem to be confronted is how best to use those resources that are freed from the defense budget. The evidence suggests that those resources could be deployed to help promote productivity growth through public investment, but competing interests will press for tax relief and spending in other areas.

Given the public sector's relatively small size, it is unrealistic to think that all the financing of projects to enhance public and human capital can come at the expense of other sectors of government. Besides defense, there are few substantial areas of funding from which public investment can draw away resources. Without additional tax revenues, a process of governmental self-cannibalization will be the likely result of an effort to increase public investment. For example, one can anticipate that in the future an initiative to increase the availability of health care for the poor and uninsured citizens in the country will stake a claim to public funds. Indeed, it can be argued that such an increase should be viewed as a further investment in human resources, since labor productivity is positively associated with good health. The point, however, is that the same temptation to find other areas to cut will present itself when public health care expands. In that context, it might be education and infrastructure that are asked to retrench. Rather than seeing public spending as a zero-sum game in which an increase in one area requires a counterproductive reduction in another, Americans should be willing to countenance real growth in public investment, which can best be financed by new taxes and forgone private consumption.

A Proposal to Raise Investment
through Changes to the Tax Code

International cross-sectional data presented earlier suggests that tax aversion in the United States might be caused by our tendency to rely more heavily on property taxation than comparable countries, our less progressive tax structure, and our inclination to spend the resources collected through taxation in ways that are not readily observable to taxpayers. U.S. polling data generally support these inferences. Thus, in thinking about the design of a tax structure which would strengthen—that is, enlarge—the public sector, the following principles should serve as a guide. Taxation in the United States should avoid increasing the property tax, minimize the income tax, and be progressive. Furthermore, the revenues collected should be dedicated to visible programs such as education and infrastructure investment so that taxpayers in this country can observe the benefits of their tax dollars at work.

Each of these principles will constrain and shape a proposed program of tax reform. The need for progressivity means that a consumption tax, though apparently viewed favorably by a majority of the public, can only be used in conjunction with other taxes that offset its regressivity. The income tax, by contrast, though progressive, tends to generate hostility. If it were possible to reduce this tax for large numbers of people, such a change might substantially overcome tax aversion, by making it more progressive. The optimum system of taxes, therefore, will combine the use of a revamped income tax with a value added tax (VAT). The first of these would reduce revenue, but at the same time become much more progressive than it is now. The VAT would raise revenue to the level desired, assuming that its implementation would not face stiff public resistance. This combination of taxes would aim to increase the tax/GDP ratio in such a way that the progressivity of the tax structure would be enhanced while increasing the relative importance of the consumption tax compared to the income tax.

Assume that all of the changes to be implemented occur at the federal level and that the objective is to find the funds to finance about $60 billion in additional public investment. The proposal presented in Table 20 accomplishes that objecitve while envisioning broad changes in the structure of the federal income tax. It would exempt from payment all those who earn $25,000 or less, reduce the income tax liability of those earning between $25,000 and $50,000 by 25 percent, hold constant the tax liability for those earning between $50,000 and $200,000, and increase by 10 percent the taxes paid by those earning more than $200,000. These changes are undertaken so as to increase the progressivity of the income tax, an essential measure to offset the regressivity of the proposed VAT. Reducing the income tax burden of those earning under $50,000 while increasing it for high earners, however, would have resulted in a net loss of about $64 billion in 1988. This shortfall, added to the revenue needed for capital investment and education, means that the proposed consumption tax must generate revenue of roughly $125 billion.

The value-added tax, similar to that in use in Canada and the European Community, is a tax that occurs at each stage of production. In principle it taxes only the value added by firms—that is, the summation of wages, interest, rents, and profits. As such it excludes from taxation the purchase of materials and capital goods by one firm from another. In practice, however, it is administered typically by taxing the total value of sales of all firms and then allowing such firms to claim a credit for taxes paid on intercompany transactions. According to the Congressional Budget Office a broadly based 5 percent VAT would in 1992 generate additional revenue of $89.4 billion, whereas one that excluded food, housing, and medical care would realize $52.1 billion.[39] Thus, it appears that in order to raise the $125 billion necessary both to offset the losses associated with the proposed changes in the income tax and at the same time raise the resources necessary to finance enhanced public investment a broadly based VAT of about 7 percent will be required.

Table 20
Calculations of Proposed Changes in Income Tax

1. Elimination of income tax
    liability for those earning
    less than $25,000   -$47.3 billion

2. 25 percent reduction in income tax
    liability for those earning
    between $25,000 and $50,000   -$26.8 billion

3. No change in income tax
    liability for those earning
    between $50,000 and $200,000   0

4. 10 percent increase in income
    tax liability for those earning
    $200,000 and above   +$10.0 billion

5. Net change in tax revenue from
    realigning income tax brackets   -$64.1 billion

Source: U.S. Department of the Treasury, Internal Revenue Service, *Statistics of Income: 1988, Individual Income Tax Returns* (Washington, D.C.: Government Printing Office, 1991), Table 1.1, p. 18.

By no means does this suggestion represent a completed version of a tax reform package.[40] It does, however, illustrate that the revenue-generating capacity of a tax on goods and services can be combined with an increase in the progressivity of the income tax to raise additional resources for financing public investment. The kind of program suggested here might well dissipate the intense tax aversion that characterizes this country. Besides shifting emphasis away from one of the most unpopular taxes and toward a moderate national consumption tax, the proposal holds out hope for reinvigorating popular faith in public-sector initiatives. It would do so through investments in education and infrastructure that promise a visible economic payoff over the long run. Enhanced public investment will augur well for a turnaround in the rate of productivity growth in this country and in the process help to raise the living standards of the American people.

NOTES

1. The fourteen OECD nations under consideration here account for more than 70 percent of the total OECD population, more than 85 percent of the GNP of all OECD countries, and upward of 88 percent of all taxes collected in the OECD. For population figures, see United Nations, *Demographic Yearbook, 1990* (New York: United Nations, 1992); for GNP figures, U.S. Department of Commerce, Bureau of the Census, *Statistical Abstract of the United States, 1991* (Washington, D.C.: Government Printing Office, 1991), Table 1445, p. 840; for tax revenue figures, *ibid.*, Table 1457, p. 846.

2. Edward F. Denison, *Accounting for Slower Economic Growth: The United States in the 1970s* (Washington, D.C.: The Brookings Institution, 1979), p. 4.

3. John H. Bishop, "Is the Test Score Decline Responsible for the Productivity Growth Decline?" *American Economic Review* 79, no. 1 (March 1989): 178.

4. Charles Schultze, "The Federal Budget and the Nation's Economic Health," in *Setting National Priorities: Policy for the Nineties*, ed. Henry J. Aaron (Washington, D.C.: The Brookings Institution, 1990), pp. 19–63; Edward M. Gramlich, "Setting National Priorities: 1992," *Journal of Economic Perspectives* 6, no. 2 (Spring 1992): 3–12.

5. The following discussion draws heavily from Louis A. Ferleger and Jay R. Mandle, "Reverse the Drain on Productivity with Mass Education and Retraining," *Challenge* 33, no. 4 (July-August 1990), pp. 17–21.

6. J. Bradford DeLong and Lawrence H. Summers, *Equipment Investment and Economic Growth*, National Bureau of Economic Research Working Paper No. 3515, Cambridge, Mass., November 1990, p. 3.

7. David Alan Aschauer, *Public Investment and Private Sector Growth: The Economic Benefits of Reducing America's 'Third Deficit,'* (Washington, D.C.: Economic Policy Institute, 1990); see also David Alan Aschauer, "Is Public Expenditure Productive?" *Journal of Monetary Economics* 23, no.2 (1989): 177–200. In addition, see Robert Heilbroner, "Lifting the Silent Depression," *New York Review of Books*, October 24, 1991, pp. 6–8.

8. Henry J. Aaron, "Discussion," in *Is There a Shortfall in Public Capital Investment?* ed. Alicia H. Munnell (Boston: Federal Reserve Bank of Boston, 1990), p. 51.

9. The authors were required to compare 1973–90 productivity data with 1975–89 tax revenue information because of problems of data availability.

10. Public physical investment covers spending for construction and rehabilitation, acquisition of major equipment, and other physical assets. For an elaboration, see *Budget of the United States Government, Fiscal Year 1993* (Washington, D.C.: Government Printing Office, 1992), section 3, pp. 35–49.

11. The authors were required to compare increases in tax revenues for 1980–89 with investment rates for 1978–88 because of problems in data availability.

12. The authors were forced to compare changes in tax revenues, excluding Social Security, for 1975–89 with investment rates for 1975–88 because of problems in data availability.

13. See Louis Ferleger and Jay R. Mandle, "Co-signs and Derivations of America's Two-Score Decline: Poor Math Skills, Poor Productivity," *Challenge* 35, no. 3 (May/June 1992), Table 1, p. 48.

14. It is possible that the decline in 1987 and subsequent years in the percentage of responses that considered the federal income tax to be the least fair was a reaction to the reduction of its progressivity that was introduced with the tax reform of 1986. A more likely explanation of this decline, however, is that it was a response to the simplification of the tax code that occurred in that year.

15. The negative sign for the effective tax rate for high-income production workers in France indicates that this group received governmental benefits in excess of its level of taxation.

16. Kevin Phillips, *The Politics of Rich and Poor: Wealth and the American Electorate in the Reagan Aftermath* (New York: Random House, 1990), p. 213.

17. Benjamin I. Page and Robert Y. Shapiro, *The Rational Public: Fifty Years of Trends in Americans' Policy Preferences* (Chicago: University of Chicago Press, 1992), pp. 163–64.

18. Page and Shapiro, *The Rational Public* p. 161.

19. Aschauer, *Public Investment and Private Sector Growth*, p. 13.

20. See, for example, David Alan Aschauer, "Why Is Infrastructure Important?" in Munnell, ed., *Is There a Shortfall in Public Capital Investment?* pp. 31, 40–48.

21. See David A. Aschauer, "Public Investment and Productivity Growth in the Group of Seven," in Federal Reserve Bank of Chicago, *Economic Perspectives* 13, no. 5 (1989): 17–25; and Alicia H. Munnell, "How Does Public Infrastructure Affect Regional Economic Performance?" in Munnell, ed., *Is There a Shortfall in Public Capital Investment?* pp. 69–103.

22. Henry J. Aaron, "Discussion," in Munnell, ed., *Is There a Shortfall in Public Capital Investment?* p. 52.

23. Charles R. Hulten, "Discussion," in *ibid.*, p. 105.

24. "Marshaling Knowledge for Development," *World Bank Policy Research Bulletin* 3, no. 2 (March-April 1992): 3.

25. U.S. Department of Commerce, Bureau of the Census, *Statistical Abstract of the United States, 1991* (Washington, D.C.: Government Printing Office, 1991), Table 214, p. 132.

26. Indeed, there was a strong statistical relationship between the rate of growth of total factor productivity from 1979 to 1988 and 1970 mathematics test results. See Ferleger and Mandle, "Co-Signs and Derivations of America's Two-Score Decline," pp. 48–50.

27. The following two paragraphs are based upon Bishop, "Is the Test Score Decline Responsible for the Productivity Growth Decline?" Quotations are from pp. 184, 193, 194.

28. Edward M. Gramlich, "Setting National Priorities: 1992," *Journal of Economic Perspectives* 6, no. 2 (Spring 1992): 7–8.

29. Aschauer, *Public Investment and Private Sector Growth*, p. 28.

30. Bishop, "Is the Test Score Decline Responsible for the Productivity Growth Decline?" p. 193.

31. Richard E. Peterson et al., *Adult Education and Training in Industrialized Countries* (New York: Praeger Publishing, 1982), p. 67. Emphasis in original.

32. Ezra F. Vogel, *Japan as Number One: Lessons for America* (Cambridge, Mass.: Harvard University Press, 1979), pp. 27, 29.

33. Nell P. Eurich, *The Learning Industry: Education for Adult Workers* (Princeton, N.J.: Carnegie Foundation for the Advancement of Teaching, 1990), pp. 9, 111.

34. For a discussion of African-Americans, see Louis Ferleger and Jay R. Mandle, "African-Americans and the Future of the U.S. Economy," *Trotter Institute Review* (Winter/Spring 1991): 3–7.

35. Richard J. Murnane, "Education and the Productivity of the Work Force: Looking Ahead," in *American Living Standards: Threats and Challenges*, eds., Robert E. Litan, Robert Z. Lawrence, and Charles Schultze (Washington, D.C.: The Brookings Institution, 1988), pp. 228–29

36. "Industrial Policy," *BusinessWeek*, April 6, 1992, pp. 73, 74.

37. Robert Eisner, "Divergences of Measurement and Theory and Some Implications for Economic Policy," *American Economic Review* 79, no. 1 (March 1989): 4–5.

38. Gramlich, "Setting National Priorities: 1992," pp. 4–5.

39. Congressional Budget Office, *Reducing the Deficit: Spending and Revenue Options*, report to the Senate and House Committees on the Budget, Part 2 (Washington, D.C.: Government Printing Office, 1990), pp. 417–18.

40. For a discussion of various tax reform proposals, see U.S. Department of the Treasury, Office of the Secretary, *Tax Reform for Fairness, Simplicity and Economic Growth*, Treasury Department Report to the President, vols. 1, 2, 3, November 1984. See also various publications by Citizens for Tax Justice; see Statement of Robert S. McIntyre before U.S. Congress, House, Committee on Ways and Means, "Concerning Middle Class Tax Relief, Tax Equity, and Fairness and the President's Anti-Growth, Tax-Shelter Initiatives," 102d Cong., 2d sess., February 5, 1992.

INDEX

ABOUT THE AUTHORS

Louis A. Ferleger is a professor of economics and chair of the department of economics at the University of Massachusetts, Boston. He has published widely in the areas of agricultural history and African American economic development. He has received numerous grants, including a National Endowment for the Humanities fellowship in 1988. He has recently edited *Agriculture and National Development: Views on the Nineteenth Century* (Iowa State University Press, 1990).

Jay R. Mandle is W. Bradford Wiley Distinguished Professor of Economics at Colgate University. He has published widely in the areas of Caribbean economic development and history and African American economic development. His most recent book is *Not Slave, Not Free: The African American Economic Experience Since the Civil War* (Duke University Press, 1992).

Since 1986 the authors have jointly worked on and written about problems of competitiveness and productivity in the American economy.